The Lady of the Lake
Had Bouffant Hair

poems by

Angie V. Clevinger

Finishing Line Press
Georgetown, Kentucky

The Lady of the Lake Had Bouffant Hair

Copyright © 2023 by Angie V. Clevinger
ISBN 979-8-88838-178-6 First Edition
All rights reserved under International and Pan-American Copyright Conventions. No part of this book may be reproduced in any manner whatsoever without written permission from the publisher, except in the case of brief quotations embodied in critical articles and reviews.

ACKNOWLEDGMENTS

"A Seat at the Table." *Artemis Journal*, XXVIII, 2021
"Before I Was Born." *Artemis Journal: Women Hold Up Half the Sky*, XXVI, 2019
"My Mountain Women Tribe." *Anthology of Appalachian Writers*, VI, 2021
"Women's Talk." *Anthology of Appalachian Writers*, VI, 2021
"Appalachian Golden Girls." *Artemis Journal*, XXIX, 2022

Publisher: Leah Huete de Maines
Editor: Christen Kincaid
Cover Art and Design: Elysia Edwards
Author Photo: Larry Clevinger II

Order online: www.finishinglinepress.com
also available on amazon.com

Author inquiries and mail orders:
Finishing Line Press
PO Box 1626
Georgetown, Kentucky 40324
USA

Table of Contents

Words from the Poet 1

Before I Was Born 3

Women's Talk 4

Vacation at the Nut House 6

Brick House 8

My Mountain Women Tribe 9

When Cousin Leslie Got Pregnant 11

Taxi Caste 12

Predictable Family Calendar 13

After the Funeral 14

Not My Momma 15

Appalachian Golden Girls 16

Will the Circle… 17

Lady of the Lake 18

Toll House Lungs 19

Rainbow Phlegm 20

Food Lion Ghost 21

Virtuous Woman 22

I Want to Make an Ashtray 23

A Seat at the Table 24

Words from the Poet

When someone dies your relationship does not end, it merely changes. My relationship with my mother took such a change when she died January 13, 2022.

I must thank my neighbors, who adopted me in a way, as an honorary grandchild. Without Granny and Pa, I doubt I would be here today. They fed me when I was hungry, bathed me when I was dirty, and taught me right from wrong.

I must thank my colorful family members, the good, the bad, and the ugly—they inspire me to write. I took creative liberties with their characters, so I could portray their true essence--I drew from emotion rather than facts only. I include in this mix my chosen family members—Michael King and the neighborhood kids. I will never run out of material.

I am all that I am because of loving caring teachers. One in particular, John Hocker, my fifth-grade teacher, believed in me and made me see that I could still love my family, but could make better choices for myself. Mr. Hocker gave me my first taste of success and I have been reaching for those big goals ever since. I must thank every teacher I ever had for working with me and teaching me.

April Asbury has been a friend of mine since high school and she is one of the best writers I have ever read. She and I write together, and she gives me feedback. We do this for each other. She's the kind of woman that revels in the success of other women. Every woman needs an April in their lives. Her partner Jack Hambly is supportive to us both.

I have two beautiful daughters, Emma and Violet. They are kind and intelligent. Violet, the youngest, is wild and free. Emma is an old soul and loves words and justice. They celebrate my successes with me. They are my cheerleaders.

My three cats Frodo, Dobby, and Thomas J. O'Malley make our home both cozy and chaotic. All of them try to help me when I type my poems by lying on the keyboard, they have quite figured out typing just yet.

I would be remiss if I did not thank Dr. Tammy Parks, Professor of Art, at New River Community College, who put me in touch with one of her students: Elysia Edwards. Elysia took all my ideas and poetry symbolism and created cover art that was beyond my highest expectations.

Last, but not least, I must thank my husband, Larry. He cheers me on when things are great, but most importantly he holds me and encourages me when times are hard. We have been in each other's lives for over 31 years, and we have been married 24 of those years. Love is not a marathon, but I believe it takes a certain amount of stubbornness to stick together. Larry and I have stubbornness in spades. He is a loving father and husband, he held down the home front for me to earn two master's degrees and write these poems.

This book would not have been possible without the village of people I just mentioned. This book is dedicated to all those people, and many more, who poured themselves into me.

Thank you.

Before I Was Born

Before I was born, I hop-scotched
on the twangy notes of a banjo.

Before my soul found a body, I floated
atop streams of corn liquor, down the
esophageal slide of a flatfooting drunkard
dancing to Foggy Mountain Breakdown.

Before I was knitted in bone and sinew,
I was the smoke swirling around bouffant bleached heads.

The only way you'd have known
I was in your mist is if you looked at the coffee cups
and discarded cigarette-butts
stained by crimsons and pinks
tattooed by mountain-women's painted lips.

In the before time, when I was asked
where I wanted to be planted, I chose
the brightest bottled blond, with the highest hair and
the reddest lips for my Momma.

Smokey me clung to Momma's polyester dress,
danced at her amply cleavage-ed breasts, and
kissed her red stained cigarette sucking lips.

Choose a Daddy, I was told, so I searched
for the man who drank amber rives of liquid corn,
his sweet vapor breath drew me near,
his laughter a sweet poison.

Before I floated in womb waters, I chose
them—'cause I can't live without
                smoke,
                              corn liquor,
                                          and the twang of a banjo.

Women's Talk

i come from mommas and aunts
sitting around an ashtray-laden table
drinking coffee
from lipstick-tattood mug rims
talking about their men
husbands,
      has-beens,
           sons,
                fathers,
                      their broke, dumb, lazy,
                          smart-ass men.

i come from silence
a kaleidoscope of bruises
peeking through carefully applied pancake
they whisper truths
bobbing their heads together
the fog engulfs them in secrecy.

i come from fields yielding
hard-won proof
they speak of birthing
what the after-birth foretold
the stretching and pushing out of life
the woeful cries determined to become
they speak of babies that were lost
their faces marble-stone
words make the lost babies real.

i come from cluttered tables of women-kin
who don't mince words
and say damn a lot
Cost-Cutter cigarettes pulled
from bright yellow cellophane packs
the flame floating on lightning bug wings
from mouth to avocado-green ashtray
and back again.

i come from magick darkness
they speak of visitations from the dearly departed
they tell of the time they held the hand of a loved one
as they walked into the other world
the smoke engulfs them as their voices rise and fall
there is a rhythm as they share their wisdom with one another.
it is a ritual i have yet to participate in
i am young and not yet a woman
i breathe the smoke
but I have not felt the fire.

Vacation At the Nut House

I overheard my Momma
tell Aunt Sandra
who'd just lost her job at the Merita Bread Store
that she could get herself a decent vacation
if she just went to her doctor
and told him she wanted to kill herself.

I made sure not to move
or breathe too hard
under the table.

I examined Momma's petite Irish red-toes
peeking out from her wedged-heels
her lilac frilled-sundress hit her just above the knee.

Cigarette smoke tickled my nose
A sneeze threatened to give away my hiding place.

>*Hell, Lana I can't check myself into St. Albans just to get a little break from my family.*

Shit! St. Albans has a bowling alley, a beauty parlor, ceramics class—I made this here ashtray we're using.

>*I don't know Lana. Don't you miss your kids when you're at the nut house?*

Well Sandra, your kids can come visit you while you're there. I mean, it's not like it's a prison. Tommy went bowling with me and Angie and Randy ate dinner with me twice a week.

>*I don't know. It seems so. . . so . . . devious. But, after losing my job, I know we ain't got no money to go no wheres. I sure could use a break.*

The pills they give you ain't bad either, if you know what I
mean, and group therapy is fun too. You meet some of the most
interesting people at St. Albans.

> You mean like Pat McCoy, the woman who shot her
> husband and his whore while they were in bed together?

Well, Sandra you can't judge Pat for that, that bitch
had that a comin'.

I wanted to pinch Momma's porcelain-smooth leg hard.

I'd worried about her.
Daddy said she was sick—
my brother Tommy got to go bowling!

My face feverish with anger
I reached out my curled fingers
ready to twist Momma's meaty milk-skin
just above the knee.

At the moment I reached to execute my torture
Momma and Sandy left the table.

*Angie? Angie? Where are you? We're gonna go to McDonald's for
ice cream. I wonder where the hell she's at?*

Damn, I missed out again.

Brick House

Them basketball boys would trip over their feet
bump their heads
and
drool
when momma wore her cheetah print
string bikini.

Them muscle car men would
honk
their
horns
when momma mowed grass in her "Daisy Dukes"
and halter top.

Monroe and Hayworth
had nothin' on momma.

My Mountain Women Tribe

My tribe consisted of women
named Loretta, Janis, Dolly, Reba, and Martina
they sang songs straight to my soul.

I could picture them sittin' around the kitchen table,
leaving lipstick tattoos on Ironstone coffee cups.

Janis would fit right in tellin' her story about a love, named Bobby
she let get away up near Salinas.

Reba would have us in tears telling how her momma,
who nicknamed her Fancy
bought her a dancin' dress and told her to be "nice" to the gentleman
they'd be proud of her for building that orphanage
for the children in her hometown.

Momma and my Aunt Patty would tell stories of their cheating men
after Loretta told how she told that tramp
Doo was with, "You Ain't Woman Enough to Take My Man."

My Aunt Sandy, who worked at the Merita Bread Store,
would have bonded with Dolly
as she complained about how hard it was to work 9 to 5
and make a livin' in a man's world.

Every bouffant head would nod and every hue of painted lips
would pull smoke deep into her lungs,
magickal smoke escaping from Winton's, Marlboros, and Virginia
Slims would quiet rising tensions
as Martina talked about how her bruised momma
one 4th of July set their house on fire
while her daddy lay asleep in a drunken stupor on the couch.

Yep, Loretta, Janis, Dolly, Reba, and Martina sang about the same wretchedness
I'd heard the women in my family talk about since I was in the womb.

These balladeer-ing women were my coven.

I imagined their stories being told around the smoky-kitchen table
they were just like my Momma, Aunt Sandy, and Aunt Patty
they just got rich singin' the stories mountain women
been tellin' for years.

When Cousin Leslie Got Pregnant

What are they doin' up there at that damned high school
that's what I'd like to know.

>Well Sandy, you know Leslie didn't get pregnant at school.

I tell ya', they go to that high school and they get knocked up
it's like something's in the water.

>It's not part of the curriculum and it's not in the water
>you know what this is about.

Are you saying my Leslie's a whore?

>No, I ain't sayin' that, hell, you and me got pregnant young.

But Leslie was my smart one. She was making A's and B's in school
Jackie and me provided her a good home, or at least better than what
we had growin' up

>It'll be okay, Sandy
>we did it
>just look at us now.

A rare silence fell over the table as both women pulled the cancerous smoke deep into their lungs.

Even from under the table, I thought I could almost hear the silent truth spoken between them.

Years later when I went to high school, I didn't drink from the water fountains, just in case.

Taxi Caste

Forget yellow, the taxi's of my youth were all colors
But owned by Blue and White
Every 3rd of the month me and momma went to town for $2.75
My fare cost a quarter

If we got the groceries and wanted to stop other places
Cost a dollar for each stop
It was another $2.75
Back then that whole trip could cost $10 in food stamps

There's a whole economy to being poor
One Xanex goes for $5
Time alone with mama--even though it was always love
A whole carton of cigarettes

The really poor and perhaps the really moral
Walked the streets

There's a caste system to poverty too
The people with new cars looked down on
The people with junky cars looked down on
the people riding Blue and White
The taxi riders looked at the those who walked
With pity and indignation.

September 1981

Sunday	Monday	Tuesday	Wednesday	Thursday	Friday	Saturday
Predictable Family Calendar		1	2	3 Checks come on the 3rd. Winstons, Virginia Slims make sweet nicotine wreathed, halos upon their laughing heads. The smell of cooking bacon, a roast in the oven, thick sausage gravy on biscuits. A bath in warm water, momma powdering me and helping me dress for bed. Sleep comes easily.	4	5
6	7	8	9	10 Wrinkles crease youngish skin, foreheads begin to show worry. I play outside morning light through dusk, the laughter is no more.	11	12
13	14	15	16	17	18	19
Putrid smells fill my nostrils: Cost Cutters, cheap generic cigarettes, two fiery lights move in the dark, devil horns emitting putrid smoke from their lit ends . Cooking cabbage, watery wienie gravy boils angrily on the stove. Dad's sausage-blotched face warns of kerosene-vapor breath. It's silence or yelling, tension like moss laden willows, joins the smoke in the air.						
20	21	22	23	24	25	26
Onion layered clothing protects me. The war rages outside my door. I snuggle, paralyzed down into the covers, pretending not to hear: the opening of the door, the breaking of the glass, the sobbing. I haven't slept in days.						
27	28	29	30			
Best hide in the closet. The bombs can't get me here. I am a warrior fighting my bowels and stomach. Trying to keep the food I have eaten down. I can make it two more days.						

After the Funeral

I hear Momma at the table talkin' to herself,

"You never loved me!"
lit cigarette dangling from shiny crimson lips

Daddy's trapped in his coffin
I remember telling the bees,

"He's dead—if you give a damn!"

Not My Momma

My Momma's hair is
a flat drab-brown these days

All her sisters are dead, except for Pattie,
and she never cared for that one

Momma's not much of a cusser these days
she lacks the breath to weave together colorful strings
of obscenities with the gusto of her 30's

She is no longer the painted lady
her face is now Martha White pale
her lips a thin line lost in a sea of face

Gone is her sass
gone is her bottle-blond bouffant hair
gone is her harlot-red lips
gone is the smoke swirling around vexed women's heads
gone is the scent of Jean Nate

I don't know who the hell this torpid
old woman is

But she ain't my Momma.

Appalachian Golden Girls

them Golden Girls weren't the first women
to sit around a table and bitch about their lives

they had cheesecake
Momma and her sisters had out of date Ding-Dongs
Aunt Sandy got free down at the Merita Bread store where she worked
what Momma and company were missing was a matriarch
there was no Sophia among them
these women lived too fast and hard

there were no Roses at their table
naivety was lost somewhere between the shedding of first blood and
the breaking of the caul

Momma's coven of sisters understood all too well the cyclical
nature of life
they chanted the raw verses of childbirth
Spells of bitchery whispered about jessabelles real and imagined

They damn sure weren't no Golden Girls
but them were the golden years
when their bouffant heads would bob in rhythm with each woman's
fleeting thoughts
their cigarettes flitting like lightning bugs to the cadence of their talk
ashtray cauldrons scattered on burnt tablecloths
held the ashes of their memories and when the scent
Jean Nate and nicotine
smoke filled the room and floated out the rusty screened window
into the summer night

Will the Circle . . .

Cylinder tobacco sticks bounce on bitching lips
painted in hues of red.

The filters stamped in scarlets shine
as bright as the lightning bug's rear-end.

The firefly that rests on the cigarette's end
is merely a puppet made to dance
to the music of punctuated syllables spewing out of puckered lips.

Momma's chest rattles deeply to the rhythm of each inhale and exhale
this beat raises energy around the circle of women.

The magick smoke rises from Virginia Slim and Winston wands
as the mountain witches speak in whispers about subjects too dark to
speak out loud.

The dark magick happens within hidden lungs
not coming to fruition for many decades to come
no bones about it, this smoky magick will someday kill this coven.

Lady of the Lake

The lake breathes like a dragon
that smokes a carton a day.
The ripples ebb and flow against the bank
permeating my brain
flipping a memory switch.

My mother becomes the Lady of the Lake
the steam off the water turns to smoke choking me.
The yellow ginko on the ridge floods my consciousness
I see Cost-Cutter cellophane labels
stuck to generic items of my childhood home bought down at the Kroger.

I frantically seek out the sword
but this is not Camelot
and this water is just
COPD phlem.

And Momma
prednisone bloated
has
drowned.

Toll House Lungs

chocolate chip cookies appeared on the screen
really a scan of momma's lungs
WebMD holds nothing back as
ethereal smoke flipped a switch in my mind
then images flood over me

momma's crimsoned tattooed filters
lie in an avocado green ashtray

red raw lung tissue matches long ago lipstick hues

green
one color of the 1970's kaleidoscope
hacked up sputum
stained on tissues

cigarette smoke circles her bouffant do

oven smoke from burnt cookies
billows out through the open kitchen windows

sun shines through wisps
creating shapes
white wings
twisted horns

smoke
it all comes back to the smoke
tragic
        deadly
                magick
                        smoke

Rainbow Phlegm

She told me when she was at the Highland Ridge Rehab

"They sure do believe in giving me the Mucinex here
I'm coughing up everything, what I'm coughing up now looks
like chocolate pudding."

Momma gave a phlegm color report every time she was sick
She would tell me the color of her sputum
Like a physician of old, I would interpret it telling her if it was allergies,
sinus, cold, flu, or pneumonia

Janus, was I, keeping the door and I would open it for her to seek medical help
Seeking medicine on yellow, green—a few antibiotics, Robitussin DM
She'd be better in a couple of weeks

But not with COVID

Now there's this new color . . . brown and the consistency of
chocolate pudding
My precognition fails me now, this Covid rainbow phlegm maker
doesn't play by the rules

Food Lion Ghost

I've been grocery shoppin' for my Momma
since I was 16 years old

I can buy what she needs
without ever looking at a list
but she writes it down anyway

When she dies I'll cling to lists of food
written in her hand
I'll place them in a box full of cards
she's sent me over the years

Then I'll cry
remembering how I begrudged her
bothered by the running of her errands

I'll remember her fondly when I purchase
Banquet Meals
Ramen noodles
Diet Sierra Mist
Bo-bo bread
and eggs

I'll smile when I'm behind someone in line
getting Pall Mall 100's in the orange pack

Momma's gonna haunt me every time
I go to the Food Lion

Virtuous Woman

Proverbs 31:10: Who can find a virtuous woman? For her price is far above rubies.

If Momma's life hadn't been poverty pocked
cascading rubies should have dripped down her neck
accentuating her ample ripe bosom

Her bleach blond bouffant would have been done at the beauty parlor
not at our kitchen table
her cascade of curls trapped with a Daisy Leather Hair stick barrette
holding it high
platform sandals showcasing my mother's pink-painted petite Irish toes
the norm if her life had been different

Momma's mouth would have never taken a draw off a Cost Cutter
Cigarette
but instead, her harlot lips would have caressed filters of Virginia Slims
her teeth would have been white
she would have worn a toothy grin

Her makeup pristine
no raccoon eyes from streaming tears
her words loving and kind
not sharp and hurtful and full of bite

I imagine her laughing,
relaxed, a smooth forehead erased of worry
nicely clothed, confident even

When she is gone from the confines of this life
I imagine this as her happy heaven

I Want to Make an Ashtray

I'll take avocado green please
yes a little burnt orange would be lovely
this pen lid will pock the surface nicely
surface it like herpy-ridden down-yonder flesh
if my soul were pottery this putrid
cigarette butt holder would be its mirror
when you feel like you can't make nothin' of your life
you go to the nut-house and make ashtrays
at least you do something useful
and when you're made enough to kill
you throw your bile-colored soul at them
you wish for jagged shards to cut the bruised parts
of your abusers from them
when your soul can hold nothing more from the ashes
that torment you, your soul spills out
as you fling the filth within its confines across the room
hitting the drunken dragon between the eyes

A Seat at The Table

These days I wear lipstick that stains my coffee cup
but I don't suck on Winston sticks
I don't have to hide under the table
I've earned my seat around the circle

I can tell the story of the lost baby
that didn't come on Valentine's Day
the heartbreak that comes with a barren womb
the pain of labor to be ended by the knife

I can whisper the messages I received
from those dearly departed souls
hovering in corners confessing their sins
and asking for forgiveness

I can relate to Dolly as I tell about the sexist boss
who shoved a French fry in my mouth
when I asked for a raise
after making me the manager
he paid the man working under me
more cause he was a man

I can whisper about the ex-boyfriend
I had in high school who left me
covered in a kaleidoscope of bruises
I can hold my own with Loretta when I
bitch about how he got another girl
pregnant while he was still dating me

I even have stories too taboo to voice
things understood through silent stares
horrors that are private
yet everybody knows

But there is no table
in which to sit now
Momma's the only one left
the evil smoking-sticks
have sucked the life right out of her

I believe soon she'll join
her sisters around the table
her hair will be a gleaming
corn-silk blonde
newly done
with no roots showing
piled high on her head with
little huzzy-curls cascading
around her face

Her lips will be crimson
leaving stains
on Ironstone cups
and name-brand cigarettes

She will sit among her sisters
and their bouffant heads
will nod and shake with
sadness and laughter
their faces will be young
their wedge heals high
their skinned slightly
kissed by the sun

And when I finally join them
at the table with my red lipstick
my auburn bouffant hair
and my sundress of yellow
our spirits will dance
on wisps of smoke
and the air will smell of Jean Nate

Angela Clevinger is a Reading Specialist in Pulaski County, Virginia with an educational career spanning over two decades. She has been published in many educational publications, giving a voice to students and teachers, presenting their needs in a public and sometimes political arena. She uses her poetry to help her heal from a trauma filled childhood and to help others find their voice and power as well. She uses humor, strength, and truth to tell her stories which journey through surviving to thriving. Angela embraces her Appalachian Culture and brings magic to the page. She lives with her husband Larry, two daughters Emma and Violet, and three cats Dobby, Frodo, and Thomas J. O'Malley.

If you would like to contact Angela to ask questions about this chapbook, you may email her at moonivy1998@gmail.com.

www.ingramcontent.com/pod-product-compliance
Lightning Source LLC
Chambersburg PA
CBHW022128090426
42743CB00008B/1056